A HOUSE IN ITS HUNGER

Other titles from Central Square Press

A HARD SUMMATION by Afaa Michael Weaver (2014)

CRACKED CALABASH by Lisa Pegram (2015)

THE NEXT VERSE POETS MIXTAPE - VOLUME ONE: THE 4 x 4 by Melanie Henderson, Fred Joiner, Lisa Pegram, Enzo Silon Surin (2016)

FEAR OF DOGS & OTHER ANIMALS by Shauna M. Morgan (2016)

A LETTER OF RESIGNATION: AN AMERICAN LIBRETTO (2017) by Enzo Silon Surin

LETTERS FROM CONGO by Danielle Legros Georges (2017)

DEPARTURE by Samuel Miranda (2017)

UNDERWORLDS by Patrick Sylvain (2018)

A HOUSE IN ITS HUNGER

poems

Jennifer Steele

CENTRAL SQUARE PRESS

All inquiries and permissions requests should be addressed to the Publisher:

Central Square Press
Lynn, Massachusetts

publisher@centralsquarepress.com
www.centralsquarepress.com

Printed in the United States of America
First Edition

ISBN-13: 978-1-941604-08-3

ISBN-10: 1-941604-08-0

Thank you to the editors of the following publication in which these poems, or versions of them, first appeared:

"Night Gossip" (published as "For the Night") & "When I Come Home Hungry," *Pittsburgh Poetry Review*

Cover art: "Sun & Soil" by Clifton Henri

Book design: Enzo Silon Surin

for Tarah
who is a sun

and for Lisa,
the spark of it all

CONTENTS

INTRODUCTION

A HOUSE IN ITS HUNGER is a collection that grapples with the intimacy of relationships behind closed doors. In this stunning debut, Jennifer Steele cleverly explores the complexities of the body as a dwelling and the compilation of emotional experiences it consumes and harbors over time.

The beauty of the collection is in its playfulness with language, where each poem successfully tackles serious subjects, some with refreshing humor, while demanding individual attention to both craft and subject. The result is an assembly and cadence that is both smart and fresh.

At its core, this suite of 13 poems is a house and also a body under renovation, one constantly shifting between acceptance and resistance of the type of depredation that often leaves one feeling like a guest in one's own body.

—Enzo Silon Surin,
Founding Editor & Publisher

a house in its hunger

Grace

My mother never liked dark meat.
She says it messes too much with her stomach,
feels funny caught around her teeth
like the chicken still has its blood.

She holds the knife and fork to the breast
of the chicken she is cooking us for dinner,
slices off the fat first, puts the excess of guilt-skin
and dark meat aside the way my grandmother taught her
to keep her figure — never more than a pinch-width
should a woman's flesh be between her own fingers.

She watches us plate our portions, estimates
how much white meat will be left for her
as she massages the insides of her forearms.

What remains of the chicken is covered
and put into the fridge until tomorrow's dinner,
but no one remembers it. Four nights later
when I cannot sleep and go to the kitchen
looking for leftovers, I find my mother
in the glow of sink light, bent over a salad plate
littered with tiny bones and scraps of underbelly
still moist enough to grease each tip of her hands.

Looking up at me she says she really doesn't like dark meat,
that it feels funny caught around her teeth, that it tastes
like blood, like the chicken still has its eyes.
And so wouldn't it be a shame, then,
to throw it away into the garbage like that
with its flesh still hung on its bones.

Wild Turkeys

The afternoon the wild turkeys showed up early
and swarmed the front yard,
I showed them my hands first.

Rose them face out
to say I didn't have what they wanted:
bread my father tossed onto our lawn alone
in the embering of weekday evenings,
the luxury of communing with animals
only hungry, which made peaceful company.

If the turkeys had been flamingoes or peacocks,
ducks even, and we were somewhere else,
like Florida, where I found small joy
in watching lizards climb villa walls
or fascination in alligators stalking in the distance,
I would have begged my father to buy more loaves.

I would have greeted each one by name
because I would have named them
like the deer and rabbits living beneath our porch;
my hands joining my father's curiosity, his tenderness,
of dispersing crumbs of *Here you go.*
I promise I am not here to hurt you.

But under a cool November sun
we were thrown together
for reasons of hunger and hunting rifles
waiting in the thick of woods, our yard
the only one without the ferocity of dogs.

I begged my father to stop attracting
what wasn't mine to care for
and shouted this much
as they crawled closer, patch-feathered,
jutting their balded, sagging necks
looking for what I couldn't give.

What would they do
when they found my palms empty
after having dragged themselves forward
each claw in the dirt asking
Where? Where? Where? You? You? You?

Dear, You

When you learn all of the faces
of each shade of sky

there's a particular gray
that brings the soft release of snow
onto snow

        when the sound of the train
        breaks the wind apart, jealous

                            like a not-yet-lover
        & the roaring   (which calls for sparks)
        can be heard for blocks

there is stillness
in the thick white coating
of a residential street

                down a long line of trees
                their branches powdered
                & bronzed

                shading city lamps
                and house lights
                set to some romantic dim.

I think of you in the untouching
of roads. There is no one

       here, but me and perhaps
       you, as thought

   as hologram beside me.
   I want to stay

   & feel the wind
   bend the necks of trees
        into its kiss, giving
        just enough shiver
        in the bones.

Night Gossip

Lately, I've been conversing with your closet,
hold pillow talk by lamplight with your hat

forgotten on the nightstand.
I ask your shoes about your day.

Your sweaters hung for night watch ask me
why they never change guard with the season.

We swap stories of being put on and taken off,
my jealousy and how lucky they all are

to be yours. I could learn to love this loneliness —
disassemble your ghost and make good use

of the bedroom's dark, eager affections,
the sheet's sympathy and its night gossip

about how many pillows it takes in
to sculpt me, a side sleeper, neck to toe,

how I choke one to cool my breasts
and nuzzle my cheek into its chests.

I keep another knee-locked for balance,
to keep the pain out of my hips.

Keep this secret, I ask,
my fashioning of you this way.

What Happens

Mommy, when the rain doesn't come
for a long time?

The earth won't make a muscle,
open all her mouths in protest of the beauty

in the beating; she sees the rain incessant,
wanting of her hardened body, passes her any cloud,

filled and ready to dump its darkening.
She doesn't want its sweat, will say

she has nothing left to give up,
brown her hair in rebellion

when she can store so much
all on her own. Drying out takes time,

so she pockets the last storm
in each follicle of tree and blade

and stem and root she beds,
and takes the sun.

She's waiting to be swallowed whole;
for the rain to miss her a little.

She won't take anything less
than the tears.

Dear, You

Years after our footsteps
have been washed away
I consider the rain coming down,
the broomstraw of each bead come and gone,
the grip of a howling wind and it's cleansing
or flooding of colorful row houses
opposite my table in a cafe
in a still open window.

To get here, I walked past
every monument
we built like a wound,
imagined that if I ran my fingers
along the brick and glass
of the convenient store doorway
we ducked into to get out of the beating
of a summer sky we never expected
to split so wide and sudden
and push us so close
that it made no sense
not make a moment for a kiss,
forget our soaking and our long distance
from home

If I kneeled down
right in the middle of the sidewalk
and pressed my cheek to the concrete
I could hold us again,

resurrect what the water only moved
and stored away in the clouds' cabinets
in case one of us came back for our lost
like a quarter, or a single earring
caught in a dustpan
and found just in time.

Spoon

Over days, I collect scattered garments
from couch cushions and bathroom floors,
pile them in bed beside me
to soak up the silence, their needing
to be washed or folded,
sniffed to remember what's clean.

I promise to gather each heap into my arms,
pick up any sock or underwear that slips and falls
for being too small and loose
and carry them to the washing machine,
not to leave them there
after the rinse and spin is done;
be prompt to the dryer
to keep them from molding
in the dark for days.

I rarely keep my word
and sustain comfort of soft pressure
of their weight against my back
no matter the chorus of scents
in protest. I cannot sleep alone

or count the number of nights
on all of the hairs of my body

since your hands crawled
along the horizon of my waist
now a belly of fleshly divots
shaded beneath the awning of my breasts,
and now without a pillow between them,
my hips swell in pain.

What these clothes don't know
is that they are all the skin to skin
I have left to fill this expanse,
the reincarnation of your shirt and pants
to drape my neck, lay across my calf and thigh,
filled with all of the clothes I want to abandon
to spread myself wide
across all this vacancy.

When I Come Home Hungry

I want your hands
breaking

lettuce
or an egg

your care
with a shell

cutting & stirring
what steams out
the day's work

its lip marks
on my blouse collar

anticipating seat
& plate
the plush night
of my body.

You ask if I've eaten
the last of the leftovers

where seasonings you love
have gone.

I've thrown them all away.

I want what you feed me
dirty-fingered

a marinated mess
of rare meat

my teeth crave;
you here & wild
in culinary fury

making a wish meal
of chopped onions
& parmesan

crumbled butter bread
& tuna no longer lost
in our cabinets

your mouth
salt-rimmed

tongue a spoon

full & asking

to tell you

how it tastes.

Where Is Your Husband?

I ate him.

Always wanted to fish and hook me
from the inside.   He lived well
on the meals I made for him: saffron soup,
couscous and apple pie,

my mother's macaroni and cheese
served on porcelain dinner plates
shined for good company.

I took up the gut of his hunger
and couldn't help myself:

                    plumped him up for years on my silences
                    in the scrubbing and washing
                    of ovens and babies,   my exit
                    from our bed each morning to work.

Feeding at the table of my torso was a ritual,
the lie and shit at the mouth about his day.

I tried boiling him last Fall
with his appetite for lobsters,
stuffed him into the scalding water.

Got as far as covering his head
with the pot top,   but his claws gripped
                           the edge. He survived
                           his drowning.

I decided on a softening, instead,
waited on the slow thaw, took his
                    but you're so warm
and brushed and baked him in lathers
of butter and sage from my two hands.
I let him think   he was eating me down
                           first.

When he was ready I sat down,
cross-legged on the kitchen floor.
Didn't need much   just fork and knife,
a long drag of the aroma to treasure the feat.

                           I bit down
and savored what I'd cooked so long
                              from love.

I watched what went into my body — so hungry,
what else was I supposed to do?

Where Is your Husband?

Like I said
I ate him all up.

As a baby, my mother mixed blood
from my brothers' wounds into my milk
to know the taste of men as defense.

My husband climbed a tree in the dead of a storm
to touch the light. He wanted to wipe his hands clean.

My husband is stuck to the bottom of my shoe.
My husband will ruin in the wash.

He was always curious about how to get inside me,
never took time to learn front doors.

My husband is double fisting a nail and hammer.
My husband has the tendency to crawl into a cast-iron duel.

He is not here, but somewhere in this belly of mine.
Pick a lock. Any lock. He was never my husband.
Can you not smell him on me?

You tell me. My husband took my heart out
to play. Pick a floor board. Any floor board.

He is holding a gun. He is wielding a sledgehammer
bigger than himself and tiring himself out.

My husband shows himself in the shape of our son's ears
who crawls into my lap and asks me to sing him to sleep.

My husband is a stray. He is playing host.
Check her purse. He has the tendency to wander

and lock himself in tiny rooms.
My husband falls asleep to his own discordant music.

My husband talks too much shit.
He has no name. He was never my husband.

I ate him. I drank him down.

He was here a minute ago
looking for me. I get lost so easily.

Dear, You

I've made good use of what's left of my heart,
garden it for the harvest of scabs I pluck and season
on the meals I've come to make
of pink hearts of men

who when they came, customized my body
into altar after altar, religions I don't pray to
and hung themselves from my hair
on the nights they were bored or lonely.

They never set me back the way they found me.
My face is now a mirror.
My face is blank for the draw.
My face is programmable.
They kneeled and dropped what they kept in their guts.

They gave me their ribs
and I collected their insecure bones in my belly.

Ask me what I like.
Yes, I let them lie down
and come out other men
but I am no dragon or fairy

or a basement,
or a chained thing
cornered in the dark.

Who told them I have magic?
I have no magic to save them.

I am not the monster.
Stop looking at me like that.

I am still a woman
who cannot save you.

My house is littered with trinkets
and my siding is a stitched quilt
of flesh they left in offering
to keep me warm while they are gone.

I hang a few bones on the door
as a warning. Last bone last: a lie.

I know what I've become.
I told you not to love me like this.

Restoration

it begins with what the ground gives up:
soil and weed by weed pulled by force

a tearing out from the littered plot
a making of a way to rest to run to take
my tea by my dressed up window.

eat and cook and feed
to make love   to rest

— dance down the grief
of losing all the *me's*
and *you's* I've been
in private;
be in communion
with the pulse
to hide my breaking
take out my breaking on
apologize   and take out the trash.

House Guest

I.

An urgent matter of a book
holding a poem
I wanted to read to you
still naked and caught
by moonlight
is when I saw her
sprawled across the window
bigger than any other spider
in my house, hung between
the ivy bordering the frame.

I called for you to *come here*
and see this. Still undressed
in the corner of my office,
you leaned in close
and she tucked in two
of her eight legs.
You called her *shy*
as you caressed the creek
of my back, my awe
of what appeared
out of nowhere.

II.

She eats before the sun comes up,
cleans and clears her plate and body.

I don't know her name. This smart spider
who spun her web between four walls
of blooming Boston Ivy.

She made her home,
which dissolves from eyes
in sunlight, inset from the wind
and lures bumble bees or ladybugs
doing their day's work
into the lush green.

I try to show her to my son
but she isn't home. *Off to work*
I say and he runs away.

I stay, squeeze my face to the glass
to try and find her. I want to know
where she hides,
where she bides her time.

III.

Leave the spiders.
They eat the bugs we don't want.

I show my son how to grab the Daddy Long-Leg
hunched in the corner of our basement
by its longest leg. Dangle it. No harm done
and set it back where I find it.

They won't bite. There is nothing to be afraid of.
I'll never let anything bad happen to you in this house.

I pinch a fleeing ant between my fingers
just like my father showed me as a girl. *See?*

IV.

She carries her home
in her body,   spits it
from her glands
in an hour's time

artisan in the build
she collaborates with the wind
to set each strand of silk

in its right place.
When the time comes
for a walking through
or a kicked up storm
to tear through what she's made
of her house, she will move on
to find other crevices   or light
poles or car windows to rebuild
her bed & kitchen   or choose
to fix cut after cut after cut.

How lucky to be her nature.
No debt on the heart
from the cost of materials
to repair the memory
of a splintered handle.
It doesn't take a spackle & palm
sander to fill the dents in her door
from the knuckling night
after night of *please*
come to bed. Her house
is made of holes. Her house
has no locked doors.

V.

Take my tea
with my spider
at the edge of dawn,
both our homes still
& quiet.

She doesn't move
and I don't talk;
feel it would be rude
to not visit my houseguest
who chose to make her home
beautiful in our window.

My home has never been cozy.
My home has been a mismatch
of throw pillows & shelving.

I admire the minimalism
of her materials, each silk thread
attaching itself to the ivy,
the intricate & polished design,
open concept of air & suspension.

How do you do it? All alone?
She twitches two legs in, then out.

VI.

I look for you now
to tell you good morning,

miss you when you are gone
and am happy when you return

to stay in the evenings
on the outside of the window

I do not open just in case
it brings down your house.

VII.

She and her web are gone.
The wind howled and took the last of the leaves
in its mouth. The stripped vines want in now —
for me to love them still,   like this,
tapping naked against the window.

ACKNOWLEDGMENTS & GRATITUDE

How could I not start by thanking Enzo Silon Surin for what has been more than a dream fulfilled, but also spirits released and affirmed. I would like to thank Melanie Henderson for the invitation to read in her home, which is where this journey began.

I would also like to thank Ebony Chinn, Keli Stewart, Yolanda J. Franklin, Najee Omar, Billie Ruffin, and Nnaemeka Anyanwu for your support and encouragement in helping me bring these poems to their truest selves. Thank you for the talk backs from ledges and for the reminders of the necessity of this work. I would like to thank the Callaloo Family. Thank you, E. Ethelbert Miller and Parneshia Jones for your mentorship and reflections on this collection. Thank you: Alison Meyers, Elizabeth Thomas, Tony Medina, Crystal Williams, and Arielle Greenberg for your mentorship as well.

I would like to thank my parents, Pamela and Roosevelt Steele for always believing in my dreams and my ability to accomplish them, and giving me the writer and poet in you. Thank you, Auntie Faith Jackson for your encouragement and investment. I would also like to thank Tarah Jarda who told me during undergrad that I could be a Poet Laureate "or something" one day. Thank you to my son, Evan, for being and inspiring my life every day.

ABOUT THE AUTHOR

JENNIFER STEELE, a native of Middletown, CT and current Chicagoan, received her MFA from Columbia College Chicago in 2008. She is the Founder and Executive Director of Revolving Door Arts, alongside her service to the young people of Chicago through her work at Chicago Public Library. She is a 2015 fellow of the Callaloo Creative Writing Workshop and her work has appeared in Pittsburgh Poetry Review, Another Chicago Magazine, Callaloo, Columbia Poetry Review, and others.

CPSIA information can be obtained
at www.ICGtesting.com
Printed in the USA
LVHW031526020519
616417LV00013B/834/P

9 781941 604083